Contents

Chocolate Chip Waffles

1 package DUNCAN HINES® Chocolate Chip Muffin Mix
¾ cup all-purpose flour
1 teaspoon baking powder
1¾ cups milk
2 eggs
5 tablespoons butter or margarine, melted
Confectioners' sugar (optional)

Rise and shine! Nothing gets kids moving in the morning like a hearty breakfast. Add a fun twist to the A.M. with these waffles, pancakes and other tasty sunrise specials.

Preheat and lightly grease waffle iron according to manufacturer's directions.

Combine muffin mix, flour and baking powder in large bowl. Add milk, eggs and melted butter. Stir until moistened, about 50 strokes. Pour batter onto center grids of preheated waffle iron. Bake according to manufacturer's directions until golden brown. Remove baked waffle carefully with fork. Repeat with remaining batter. Dust lightly with sugar, if desired. Top with fresh fruit, syrup, grated chocolate or whipped cream, if desired.

Makes 10 to 12 waffles

Chocolate Chip Waffles

Breakfast Pizza

1 can (10 ounces) refrigerated biscuit dough
½ pound bacon slices
2 tablespoons butter or margarine
2 tablespoons all-purpose flour
¼ teaspoon salt
⅛ teaspoon black pepper
1½ cups milk
½ cup (2 ounces) shredded sharp Cheddar
  cheese
¼ cup sliced green onions
¼ cup chopped red bell pepper

Preheat oven to 350°F. Spray 13×9-inch baking dish with nonstick cooking spray.

Separate biscuit dough and arrange in rectangle on lightly floured surface. Roll into 14×10-inch rectangle. Place in prepared dish; pat edges up sides of dish. Bake 15 minutes. Remove from oven and set aside.

Meanwhile, place bacon in single layer in large skillet; cook over medium heat until crisp. Remove from skillet; drain on paper towels. Crumble and set aside.

Melt butter in medium saucepan over medium heat. Stir in flour, salt and black pepper until smooth. Gradually stir in milk; cook and stir until thickened. Stir in cheese until melted. Spread sauce evenly over baked crust. Arrange bacon, green onions and bell pepper over sauce.

Bake, uncovered, 20 minutes or until crust is golden brown.

Makes 6 servings

Breakfast Pizza

Bunny Pancakes with Strawberry Butter

Strawberry Butter (recipe follows)
2 cups buttermilk baking mix
1 cup milk
2 eggs
$\frac{1}{2}$ cup plain yogurt
Assorted candies

1. Prepare Strawberry Butter; set aside. Preheat electric skillet or griddle to 375°F.

2. Combine baking mix, milk, eggs and yogurt in medium bowl; mix well. Spoon scant $\frac{1}{2}$ cup batter into skillet. With back of spoon, gently spread batter into 4-inch circle. Spoon about 2 tablespoons batter onto top edge of circle for head. Using back of spoon, spread batter from head to form bunny ears as shown in photo.

3. Cook until bubbles on surface begin to pop and top of pancake appears dry; turn pancake over. Cook until done, 1 to 2 minutes. Decorate with candies as shown in photo.

4. Repeat with remaining batter. Serve warm with Strawberry Butter.
Makes about 12 (8-inch) pancakes

Strawberry Butter: Place 1 package (3 ounces) cream cheese and $\frac{1}{2}$ cup softened butter in food processor or blender; process until smooth. Add $\frac{1}{3}$ cup sugar; process until combined. Add $1\frac{1}{2}$ cups fresh or thawed frozen strawberries; process until finely chopped.

Reindeer Pancakes: Prepare batter as directed. Spoon scant $\frac{1}{4}$ cup batter into skillet. Quickly spread batter with back of spoon to form antlers as shown in photo. Cook as directed. Decorate as shown in photo. Serve as directed.

Top to bottom: Reindeer Pancake, Bunny Pancake with Strawberry Butter

Peanut Butter & Banana Wake-up Shake

1 cup (8 ounces) vanilla yogurt
1 cup milk
⅓ cup SKIPPY® Creamy Peanut Butter
¼ cup KARO® Light or Dark Corn Syrup
1 ripe banana, cut in chunks
5 ice cubes

1. In blender combine yogurt, milk, peanut butter, corn syrup and banana; process until smooth.

2. With blender running, gradually add ice cubes. Blend until thickened and smooth. Serve immediately.

Makes about 4 (8-ounce) servings

Prep Time: 5 minutes

Breakfast Blossoms

1 (12-ounce) can buttermilk biscuits (10 biscuits)
¾ cup SMUCKER'S® Strawberry Preserves
¼ teaspoon ground cinnamon
¼ teaspoon ground nutmeg

Grease ten 2½- or 3-inch muffin cups. Separate dough into 10 biscuits. Separate each biscuit into 3 even sections or leaves. Stand 3 sections evenly around sides and bottom of cup, overlapping slightly. Press dough edges firmly together.

Combine preserves, cinnamon and nutmeg; place scant tablespoonful in center of each cup.

Bake at 375°F for 10 to 12 minutes or until lightly browned. Cool slightly before removing from pan. Serve warm.   *Makes 10 rolls*

French Toast Sticks

1 cup EGG BEATERS® Healthy Real Egg
    Product
⅓ cup skim milk
1 teaspoon ground cinnamon
1 teaspoon vanilla extract
2 tablespoons FLEISCHMANN'S® Original
    Margarine, divided
16 (4×1×1-inch) sticks day-old white bread
    Powdered sugar, optional
    Maple-flavored syrup, optional

In shallow bowl, combine Egg Beaters®, milk, cinnamon and vanilla.

In large nonstick griddle or skillet, over medium-high heat, melt 2 teaspoons margarine. Dip bread sticks in egg mixture to coat; transfer to griddle. Cook sticks on each side until golden, adding remaining margarine as needed. Dust lightly with powdered sugar and serve with syrup, if desired. *Makes 4 servings*

Prep Time: 15 minutes
Cook Time: 18 minutes

Breakfast Baskets

8 (6-inch) flour tortillas, divided
4 tablespoons butter, melted and divided
4 bacon slices, cut into 1-inch pieces
½ cup chopped green bell pepper
½ cup chopped red bell pepper
3 tablespoons chopped onion
4 eggs
3 tablespoons milk
¼ teaspoon hot pepper sauce (optional)
¼ teaspoon salt
⅛ teaspoon black pepper

1. Preheat oven to 350°F.

2. Brush 6 tortillas with melted butter; let stand until pliable, about 5 minutes. Gently ease buttered tortillas into 6 small custard cups.

3. For handles, cut each of both remaining tortillas into 3 (1-inch) strips. (There should be 6 strips.) Brush with remaining butter. Invert muffin pan; arrange 2 strips in "u" shape around bottoms of each of 3 cups. Bake tortilla cups and handles 10 to 15 minutes or until golden brown. Remove cups and handles to wire rack; cool.

4. Meanwhile, cook bacon in medium skillet over medium-high heat until crisp, stirring occasionally. Remove bacon from skillet; set aside. Pour off all but 1 tablespoon bacon fat from skillet. Add bell peppers and onion to skillet; cook and stir until crisp-tender.

5. Whisk together eggs, milk, hot pepper sauce, salt and pepper. Add to vegetable mixture in skillet; cook and stir until eggs are set. Stir in bacon. Divide egg mixture evenly among prepared baskets. Place handles in baskets. Serve warm. *Makes 6 servings*

Breakfast Baskets

Cinnamon-Raisin Rolls

1 package (16 ounces) hot roll mix, plus
    ingredients to prepare mix
⅓ cup raisins
4 tablespoons butter, softened and divided
¼ cup granulated sugar
2 teaspoons ground cinnamon
½ teaspoon ground nutmeg
1½ cups powdered sugar
1 to 2 tablespoons fat-free (skim) milk
½ teaspoon vanilla

1. Preheat oven to 375°F. Spray 13×9-inch baking pan with nonstick cooking spray.

2. Prepare hot roll mix according to package directions; mix in raisins. Knead dough on lightly floured surface until smooth and elastic, about 5 minutes. Cover dough with plastic wrap; let stand 5 minutes.

3. Roll out dough on floured surface to 16×10-inch rectangle. Spread dough with 2 tablespoons butter. Combine granulated sugar, cinnamon and nutmeg in small bowl; sprinkle evenly over dough. Roll up dough starting at long end. Pinch edge of dough to seal.

4. Gently stretch sealed dough until 18 inches long. Cut dough into 1-inch pieces; place, cut side up, in prepared pan. Cover pan loosely with towel. Let stand 20 to 30 minutes or until doubled in size.

5. Bake 20 to 25 minutes or until golden. Cool in pan on wire rack 2 to 3 minutes. Remove from pan; cool on wire rack.

6. Combine powdered sugar, remaining 2 tablespoons butter, 1 tablespoon milk and vanilla in medium bowl. Add additional 1 tablespoon milk to make thin glaze, if desired. Spread glaze over warm rolls.   *Makes 1½ dozen rolls*

Cinnamon-Raisin Rolls

Breakfast Waffle Club Sandwich with Honey Apple Syrup

¾ cup honey, divided
¼ cup apple juice
2 tablespoons butter or margarine
2 crisp, red apples, cored and sliced
8 frozen waffles, toasted
8 thin slices ham

To prepare syrup, place ½ cup honey and apple juice in small saucepan over medium heat; heat through. Set aside and keep warm. Melt butter with remaining ¼ cup honey in large nonstick skillet over medium-high heat. Add apples; cook and stir about 4 minutes or until apples are lightly caramelized and crisp-tender. For each serving, place 2 waffles on plate, overlapping slightly. Top each waffle with 1 slice ham. Top with ¼ of apple mixture and drizzle with ¼ of syrup. *Makes 4 servings*

Favorite recipe from **National Honey Board**

Breakfast Waffle Club Sandwich with Honey Apple Syrup

Silly Snacks

Move over, milk and cookies! Your kids will gobble up these fun and filling munchies. Refuel empty tummies with smoothies, snack mixes, dips and much more.

Pizza Snack Cups

1 can (12 ounces) refrigerated biscuits (10 biscuits)
½ pound ground beef
1 jar (14 ounces) RAGÚ® Pizza Quick® Sauce
½ cup shredded mozzarella cheese (about 2 ounces)

1. Preheat oven to 375°F. In 12-cup muffin pan, evenly press each biscuit in bottom and up side of each cup; chill until ready to fill.

2. In 10-inch skillet, brown ground beef over medium-high heat; drain. Stir in Ragú Pizza Quick Sauce and heat through.

3. Evenly spoon beef mixture into prepared muffin cups. Bake 15 minutes. Sprinkle with cheese and bake an additional 5 minutes or until cheese is melted and biscuits are golden. Let stand 5 minutes. Gently remove pizza cups from muffin pan and serve. *Makes 10 pizza cups*

Prep Time: 10 minutes
Cook Time: 25 minutes

Pizza Snack Cups

Purple Cow Jumped Over the Moon

> 3 cups vanilla nonfat frozen yogurt
> 1 cup reduced-fat (2%) milk
> ½ cup thawed frozen grape juice concentrate
>   (undiluted)
> 1½ teaspoons lemon juice

Place yogurt, milk, grape juice concentrate and lemon juice in food processor or blender container; process until smooth. Serve immediately.   *Makes 8 (½-cup) servings*

Razzmatazz Shake: Place 1 quart vanilla nonfat frozen yogurt, 1 cup vanilla nonfat yogurt and ¼ cup chocolate syrup in food processor or blender container; process until smooth. Pour ½ of mixture evenly into 12 glasses; top with ½ of (12-ounce) can root beer. Fill glasses equally with remaining yogurt mixture; top with remaining root beer. Makes 12 (⅔-cup) servings.

Sunshine Shake: Place 1 quart vanilla nonfat frozen yogurt, 1⅓ cups orange juice, 1 cup fresh or thawed frozen raspberries and 1 teaspoon sugar in food processor or blender container; process until smooth. Pour into 10 glasses; sprinkle with ground nutmeg. Makes 10 (½-cup) servings.

Orange Smoothies

> 1 cup fat-free vanilla ice cream or fat-free vanilla
>   frozen yogurt
> ¾ cup low-fat (1%) milk
> ¼ cup frozen orange juice concentrate

1. Combine ice cream, milk and orange juice concentrate in food processor or blender; process until smooth.

2. Pour mixture into 2 glasses; garnish as desired. Serve immediately.   *Makes 2 servings*

Purple Cow Jumped Over the Moon

Super Nachos

12 large baked low-fat tortilla chips (about
  1½ ounces)
½ cup (2 ounces) shredded reduced-fat Cheddar
  cheese
¼ cup fat-free refried beans
2 tablespoons chunky salsa

1. Arrange chips in single layer on large microwavable plate. Sprinkle cheese evenly over chips.

2. Spoon beans over chips; top with salsa.

3. Microwave at MEDIUM (50%) 1½ minutes; rotate dish. Microwave 1 to 1½ minutes or until cheese is melted.

Makes 2 servings

Conventional Directions: Substitute foil-covered baking sheet for microwavable plate. Assemble nachos as directed on prepared baking sheet. Bake at 350°F 10 to 12 minutes or until cheese is melted.

Cook's Tip: For a single serving of nachos, arrange 6 large tortilla chips on microwavable plate; top with ¼ cup cheese, 2 tablespoons beans and 1 tablespoon salsa. Microwave at MEDIUM (50%) 1 minute; rotate dish. Continue to microwave 30 seconds to 1 minute or until cheese is melted.

Super Nachos

Honey Popcorn Clusters

Vegetable cooking spray
6 cups air-popped popcorn
⅔ cup DOLE® Golden or Seedless Raisins
½ cup DOLE® Chopped Dates or Pitted Dates,
   chopped
⅓ cup DOLE® Slivered Almonds (optional)
⅓ cup packed brown sugar
¼ cup honey
2 tablespoons margarine
¼ teaspoon baking soda

• Line bottom and sides of 13×9-inch baking pan with large sheet of aluminum foil. Spray foil with vegetable cooking spray.

• Stir together popcorn, raisins, dates and almonds in foil-lined pan.

• Combine brown sugar, honey and margarine in small saucepan. Bring to boil over medium heat, stirring constantly; reduce heat to low. Cook 5 minutes. *Do not stir.* Remove from heat.

• Stir in baking soda. Pour evenly over popcorn mixture, stirring quickly to coat mixture evenly.

• Bake at 300°F 12 to 15 minutes or until mixture is lightly browned, stirring once halfway through baking time.

• Lift foil from pan; place on cooling rack. Cool popcorn mixture completely; break into clusters. Popcorn can be stored in airtight container up to 1 week.   *Makes 7 cups*

Prep Time: 20 minutes
Bake Time: 15 minutes

Pepperoni Pizza Dip

1 cup RAGÚ® Old World Style® Pasta Sauce
1 cup RAGÚ® Cheese Creations!® Classic
    Alfredo Sauce
1 cup shredded mozzarella cheese (about
    4 ounces)
¼ to ½ cup finely chopped pepperoni

1. In 2-quart saucepan, heat Ragú Pasta Sauces, cheese and pepperoni, stirring occasionally, 10 minutes or until cheese is melted.

2. Pour into 1½-quart casserole or serving dish and serve, if desired, with breadsticks, sliced Italian bread or crackers.

Makes 3½ cups dip

Prep Time: 5 minutes
Cook Time: 10 minutes

Philadelphia® Fruit Dip

1 package (8 ounces) PHILADELPHIA® Cream
    Cheese, softened
1 container (8 ounces) strawberry or any
    flavored yogurt

MIX cream cheese and yogurt with electric mixer on medium speed until well blended. Refrigerate.

SERVE with assorted fresh fruit.

Makes about 1⅔ cups

Prep Time: 5 minutes plus refrigerating

Super Spread Sandwich Stars

1 Red or Golden Delicious apple, peeled, cored
    and coarsely chopped
1 cup roasted peanuts
⅓ cup honey
1 tablespoon lemon juice
1 teaspoon ground cinnamon
    Sliced sandwich bread

For Super Spread, place chopped apple, peanuts, honey, lemon juice and cinnamon in food processor or blender. Pulse food processor several times until ingredients start to blend, occasionally scraping down the sides with rubber spatula. Process 1 to 2 minutes until mixture is smooth and spreadable.

For Sandwich Stars, use butter knife to spread about 1 tablespoon Super Spread on 2 slices of bread. Stack them together, spread side up. Top with third slice bread. Place cookie cutter on top of sandwich; press down firmly and evenly. Leaving cookie cutter in place, remove excess trimmings with your fingers or a butter knife. Remove cookie cutter.

Makes 1¼ cups spread (enough for about 10 sandwiches)

Favorite recipe from **Texas Peanut Producers Board**

Super Spread Sandwich Stars

Creamy Taco Dip

1 pound (16 ounces) VELVEETA® Pasteurized
  Prepared Cheese Product, cut up
1 container (16 ounces) BREAKSTONE'S® or
  KNUDSEN® Sour Cream
1 package (1¼ ounces) TACO BELL® HOME
  ORIGINALS™ Taco Seasoning Mix

Microwave all ingredients in 2-quart microwavable bowl on HIGH 5 minutes or until Velveeta is melted, stirring after 3 minutes. Serve hot or cold with corn chips or tortilla chips.   *Makes 3½ cups*

Prep Time: 5 minutes
Microwave Time: 5 minutes

Tuna 'n' Celery Sticks

4 ounces cream cheese, softened
3 tablespoons plain yogurt or mayonnaise
1½ teaspoons dried basil
1 can (12 ounces) STARKIST® Solid White or
  Chunk Light Tuna, drained and flaked
½ cup finely grated carrot or zucchini
½ cup finely shredded Cheddar cheese
2 teaspoons instant minced onion
10 to 12 celery stalks, cleaned and strings
  removed

In large bowl, mix together cream cheese, yogurt and basil until smooth. Add tuna, carrot, Cheddar cheese and onion; mix well. Spread mixture into celery stalks; cut into fourths.

Makes 40 servings

Prep Time: 10 minutes

Creamy Taco Dip

Sassy Southwestern Veggie Wraps

½ cup diced zucchini
½ cup diced red or yellow bell pepper
½ cup frozen corn, thawed
1 jalapeño pepper,* seeded and chopped
(optional)
¾ cup shredded reduced-fat Mexican cheese
blend
3 tablespoons prepared salsa or picante sauce
2 (8-inch) flour tortillas

Jalapeño peppers can sting and irritate the skin; wear rubber gloves when handling peppers and do not touch eyes. Wash hands after handling.

1. Combine zucchini, bell pepper, corn and jalapeño pepper, if desired, in small bowl. Stir in cheese and salsa; mix well.

2. Soften tortillas according to package directions. Spoon vegetable mixture down center of tortillas; roll up burrito style. Serve wraps cold or warm.*   *Makes 2 servings*

To warm each wrap, cover loosely with plastic wrap and microwave at HIGH 40 to 45 seconds or until cheese is melted.

Peanut Butter 'n' Chocolate Chips Snack Mix

6 cups bite-size crisp corn, rice or wheat squares
cereal
3 cups miniature pretzels
2 cups toasted oat cereal rings
1 cup raisins or dried fruit bits
1 cup HERSHEY'S Semi-Sweet Chocolate Chips
1 cup REESE'S® Peanut Butter Chips

Stir together all ingredients in large bowl. Store in airtight container at room temperature.   *Makes 14 cups snack mix*

Sassy Southwestern Veggie Wrap

Inside-Out Turkey Sandwiches

2 tablespoons cream cheese
2 tablespoons pasteurized process cheese
   spread
2 teaspoons chopped green onion tops
1 teaspoon prepared mustard
12 thin round slices turkey breast or smoked
   turkey breast
4 large pretzel logs or unsalted breadsticks

1. Combine cream cheese, process cheese spread, green onion and mustard in small bowl; mix well.

2. Arrange 3 turkey slices on large sheet of plastic wrap, overlapping slices in center. Spread ¼ of cream cheese mixture evenly onto turkey slices, covering slices completely. Place 1 pretzel at bottom edge of turkey slices; roll up turkey around pretzel. (Be sure to keep all 3 turkey slices together as you roll them around pretzel.)

3. Repeat with remaining ingredients. *Makes 4 servings*

Original Ranch® Snack Mix

8 cups Kellogg's® Crispix® cereal
2½ cups small pretzels
2½ cups bite-size Cheddar cheese crackers
   (optional)
3 tablespoons vegetable oil
1 packet (1 ounce) Hidden Valley® Original
   Ranch® Dressing Mix

Combine cereal, pretzels and crackers in large plastic bag. Pour oil over mixture and toss to coat. Add dressing mix; toss again until coated. *Makes about 10 cups*

Inside-Out Turkey Sandwiches

Frozen Chocolate-Covered Bananas

2 ripe medium bananas
4 wooden sticks
½ cup low-fat granola cereal without raisins
⅓ cup hot fudge sauce, at room temperature

1. Cover baking sheet or 15×10-inch jelly-roll pan with waxed paper; set aside.

2. Peel bananas; cut each in half crosswise. Insert wooden stick into center of cut end of each banana about 1½ inches into banana half. Place on prepared baking sheet; freeze until firm, at least 2 hours.

3. Place granola in large plastic food storage bag; crush slightly using rolling pin or meat mallet. Transfer granola to shallow plate. Place fudge sauce in a shallow dish.

4. Working with 1 banana at a time, place frozen banana in fudge sauce; turn banana and spread fudge sauce evenly onto banana with small rubber scraper. Immediately place banana on plate with granola; turn to coat lightly. Return to baking sheet in freezer. Repeat with remaining bananas.

5. Freeze until fudge sauce is very firm, at least 2 hours. Place on small plates; let stand 5 minutes before serving.   *Makes 4 servings*

Berry Striped Pops

　　2 cups strawberries
　　¾ cup honey,* divided
　　6 kiwifruit, peeled and sliced
　　2 cups sliced peaches
　　12 (3-ounce) paper cups or popsicle molds
　　12 popsicle sticks

*Honey should not be fed to infants under one year of age. Honey is a safe and wholesome food for older children and adults.

Purée strawberries with ¼ cup honey in blender or food processor. Divide mixture evenly between 12 cups or popsicle molds. Freeze about 30 minutes or until firm. Meanwhile, rinse processor; purée kiwifruit with ¼ cup honey. Repeat process with peaches and remaining ¼ cup honey. When strawberry layer is firm, pour kiwifruit purée into molds. Insert popsicle sticks and freeze about 30 minutes or until firm. Pour peach purée into molds and freeze until firm and ready to serve.　　　　　　　　　　　　　　*Makes 12 servings*

Favorite recipe from **National Honey Board**

Super Suppers

Chef Doug

Cook up some fun for dinner tonight! Whether it's pizza or pasta, sandwiches or sides, the whole family will love these recipes (and the kids might even eat their broccoli).

Hot Diggity Dots & Twisters

⅔ cup milk
2 tablespoons margarine
  or butter
1 (4.8-ounce) package
  PASTA RONI® Four
  Cheese Flavor with
  Corkscrew Pasta
1½ cups frozen peas
4 hot dogs, cut into
  ½-inch pieces
2 teaspoons mustard

1. In large saucepan, bring 1¼ cups water, milk and margarine just to a boil.

2. Stir in pasta, peas and Special Seasonings; return to a boil. Reduce heat to medium. Gently boil uncovered, 7 to 8 minutes or until pasta is tender, stirring occasionally.

3. Stir in hot dogs and mustard. Let stand 3 to 5 minutes before serving.
                    Makes 4 servings

Prep Time: 5 minutes
Cook Time: 15 minutes

Hot Diggity Dots & Twisters

Sausage Cheeseburger Pizza

1 pound BOB EVANS® Original Recipe Roll
   Sausage
1 (12-inch) prepared pizza shell
½ cup yellow mustard
2 cups (8 ounces) shredded mozzarella cheese
½ cup chopped onion
15 dill pickle slices
¾ cup (3 ounces) shredded Cheddar cheese

Preheat oven to 425°F. Crumble and cook sausage in medium skillet
until browned; drain well on paper towels. Place pizza shell on lightly
greased 12-inch pizza pan or baking sheet. Spread mustard over
shell; top with mozzarella cheese, sausage and onion. Place pickle
slices evenly on top; sprinkle with Cheddar cheese. Bake 12 minutes
or until crust is cooked through and cheese is bubbly. Cut into thin
wedges or squares and serve hot. Refrigerate leftovers.

Makes 8 servings

Green Beans Orange

1 pound fresh *or* 2 (9-ounce) packages frozen
   whole green beans
¼ cup SMUCKER'S® Low Sugar Orange
   Marmalade
1 teaspoon lemon juice

Cut ends off green beans; wash. Cover and cook in a small amount of
boiling salted water until tender-crisp, about 5 minutes. Drain. (Or
cook frozen green beans according to package directions; drain.)

Add marmalade and lemon juice. Cook and gently stir until beans are
coated and hot. *Makes 6 servings*

Sausage Cheeseburger Pizza

Cheesy Tuna Mac

8 ounces uncooked elbow macaroni
2 tablespoons margarine or butter
2 tablespoons all-purpose flour
1 teaspoon paprika
¼ teaspoon salt
1 cup canned reduced-sodium chicken broth
6 ounces reduced-fat reduced-sodium cheese
    spread, cut into cubes
1 can (6 ounces) tuna packed in water, drained
    and flaked

1. Cook macaroni according to package directions, omitting salt. Drain; set aside.

2. Melt margarine in medium saucepan over medium heat. Add flour, paprika and salt; cook and stir 1 minute. Add broth; bring to a simmer for 2 minutes or until sauce thickens.

3. Add cheese spread; cook and stir until cheese melts. Combine tuna and pasta in medium bowl; pour sauce mixture over tuna mixture; toss to coat. Garnish with additional paprika, if desired.

Makes 4 servings

Cheesy Tuna Mac

Sweet and Sour Chicken Nuggets

2 (1-cup) bags UNCLE BEN'S® Brand
    Boil-in-Bag Rice
1 package (10 ounces) frozen chicken nuggets
    or chicken chunks
1 tablespoon oil
2 large green bell peppers, cut into 1-inch
    squares
2 large carrots, diagonally cut into thin slices
1½ teaspoons minced garlic
2 cans (8 ounces each) pineapple chunks in
    juice, drained and ½ cup juice reserved
1 jar (10 ounces) sweet and sour sauce

1. Cook rice according to package directions.

2. Prepare chicken nuggets according to package directions for conventional oven.

3. Heat oil in large skillet over medium-high heat until hot. Add bell peppers, carrots and garlic; cook and stir 4 minutes. Add reserved pineapple juice. Cover; reduce heat and simmer 10 to 12 minutes until vegetables are almost tender. Add pineapple chunks; cover and cook 2 minutes. Stir in sweet and sour sauce; cover and cook 2 more minutes or until hot.

4. Place warm chicken nuggets on a bed of rice and top with vegetable mixture. *Makes 4 servings*

Funny Face Pizzas

1 package (10 ounces) refrigerated pizza dough
1 cup pizza sauce
1 cup (4 ounces) shredded mozzarella cheese
   Assorted toppings: pepperoni, black olive
      slices, green or red bell pepper slices,
      mushroom slices
⅓ cup shredded Cheddar cheese

Heat oven to 425°F. Spray baking sheet with nonstick cooking spray; set aside.

Remove dough from package. *Do not unroll dough.* Slice dough into 4 equal pieces. Knead each piece of dough until ball forms. Pat or roll each ball into 4-inch disk. Place disks on prepared baking sheet.

Spread ¼ cup sauce on each disk. Sprinkle with mozzarella cheese. Decorate with toppings to create faces. Sprinkle with Cheddar cheese to resemble hair.

Bake 10 minutes or until cheese is just melted and bottoms of pizzas are light brown. *Makes 4 servings*

SPAM™ Sticks

1 (12-ounce) can SPAM® Luncheon Meat
1 egg
2 tablespoons milk
2 tablespoons all-purpose flour
½ cup soda cracker crumbs

Heat oven to 375°F. Slice SPAM® into 8 pieces; cut each slice in half lengthwise. Beat together egg and milk. Coat each SPAM® slice with flour. Dip in milk mixture and roll in cracker crumbs. Place on baking sheet. Bake 15 to 18 minutes or until golden brown. Serve with tartar sauce or ketchup. *Makes 4 servings*

Hearty BBQ Beef Sandwiches

1 envelope LIPTON₀ RECIPE SECRETS® Onion
   Soup Mix
2 cups water
½ cup chili sauce
¼ cup firmly packed light brown sugar
1 (3-pound) boneless chuck roast
8 kaiser rolls or hamburger buns, toasted

1. Preheat oven to 325°F. In Dutch oven or 5-quart heavy ovenproof saucepot, combine soup mix, water, chili sauce and sugar; add roast.

2. Cover and bake 3 hours or until roast is tender.

3. Remove roast; reserve juices. Bring reserved juices to a boil over high heat. Boil 4 minutes.

4. Meanwhile, with fork, shred roast. Stir roast into reserved juices and simmer, stirring frequently, 1 minute. Serve on rolls.

Makes 8 servings

Recipe Tip: Always measure brown sugar in a dry measure cup and pack down firmly. To soften hardened brown sugar, place in glass dish with 1 slice of bread. Cover with plastic wrap and microwave at HIGH 30 to 40 seconds. Let stand 30 seconds; stir. Remove bread.

Hearty BBQ Beef Sandwich

Amigo Pita Pocket Sandwiches

1 pound ground turkey
1 can (7 ounces) whole kernel corn, drained
1 can (6 ounces) tomato paste
½ cup water
½ cup chopped green bell pepper
1 package (1.0 ounce) LAWRY'S® Taco Spices
    & Seasonings
8 pita breads
    Curly lettuce leaves
    Shredded cheddar cheese

In large skillet, brown ground turkey until no longer pink; drain fat.
Add corn, tomato paste, water, green pepper and Taco Spices &
Seasonings; mix well. Bring to a boil over medium-high heat; reduce
heat to low and cook, uncovered, 15 minutes. Cut off top quarter of
pita breads and open to form pockets. Line each with lettuce leaves.
Spoon about ½ cup filling into each pita bread and top with cheese.

Makes 8 servings

Serving Suggestion: Serve with vegetable sticks and fresh fruit.

Campbell's® Cheesy Broccoli

1 can (10¾ ounces) CAMPBELL'S® Condensed Cheddar
    Cheese Soup
¼ cup milk
4 cups frozen broccoli cuts

1. In 2-quart microwave-safe casserole mix soup and milk. Add
broccoli.

2. Cover and microwave on HIGH 8 minutes or until broccoli is
tender-crisp, stirring once during heating.   *Makes 4 servings*

Prep/Cook Time: 10 minutes

Amigo Pita Pocket Sandwiches

Beefy Bread

1½ pounds ground beef
¼ cup finely chopped onion
8 ounces rotini pasta
6 tablespoons butter or margarine
⅓ cup flour
½ teaspoon pepper
¼ teaspoon salt
2½ cups milk
⅓ pound pasteurized process cheese spread, cut into cubes
1 can (4 ounces) carrots, drained
1 can (4 ounces) peas, drained
1 loaf Italian bread
   Butter or margarine, softened
   Garlic powder to taste
½ cup chopped green onions

In skillet, brown ground beef with onion. Drain. Meanwhile, cook rotini according to package directions; drain. In large saucepan, melt 6 tablespoons butter over medium heat. Stir in flour, pepper and salt. Remove from heat and gradually add milk, stirring constantly. Return to heat and add process cheese spread, stirring constantly until process cheese spread melts and sauce thickens. Add rotini, ground beef, carrots and peas to cheese sauce and keep hot.

Hollow out inside of bread loaf. Butter inside of loaf and sprinkle with garlic powder. Fill loaf with rotini mixture, wrap in foil and bake at 350°F for 15 to 20 minutes. Remove foil, cut into slices and garnish with green onions. *Makes 6 to 8 servings*

Favorite recipe from **North Dakota Beef Commission**

Cheeseburger Calzones

1 pound ground beef
1 medium onion, chopped
½ teaspoon salt
1 jar (26 to 28 ounces) RAGÚ® Hearty
    Robusto!™ Pasta Sauce
1 jar (8 ounces) marinated mushrooms, drained
    and chopped (optional)
1 cup shredded Cheddar cheese (about
    4 ounces)
1 package (2 pounds) frozen pizza dough,
    thawed

1. Preheat oven to 375°F. In 12-inch skillet, brown ground beef with onion and salt over medium-high heat; drain. Stir in 1 cup Ragú Pasta Sauce, mushrooms and cheese.

2. On floured board, cut each pound of dough into 4 pieces; press to form 6-inch circles. Spread ½ cup beef mixture on each dough circle; fold over and pinch edges to close.

3. With large spatula, gently arrange on cookie sheets. Bake 25 minutes or until golden. Serve with remaining sauce, heated.

Makes 8 servings

Prep Time: 15 minutes
Cook Time: 25 minutes

Cowboy Burgers

1 pound ground beef
½ teaspoon LAWRY'S® Seasoned Salt
½ teaspoon LAWRY'S® Seasoned Pepper
2 tablespoons plus 2 teaspoons butter OR
    margarine
1 large onion, thinly sliced
1 package (1.0 ounces) LAWRY'S® Taco Spices
    & Seasonings
4 slices cheddar cheese
4 Kaiser rolls
    Lettuce leaves
    Tomato slices

In medium bowl, combine ground beef, Seasoned Salt and Seasoned Pepper; shape into four patties. Grill or broil to desired doneness (about 5 to 6 minutes on each side for medium). Meanwhile, in medium skillet, melt butter. Add onion and Taco Spices & Seasonings; mix well. Cook onion over medium-high heat until soft and transparent. Top each patty with onions and cheese. Return to grill or broiler until cheese is melted. Place each patty on roll; top with lettuce and tomato. *Makes 4 servings*

Serving Suggestion: Serve with baked beans.

Cowboy Burger

Tic-Tac-Toe Tuna Pizza

1 bread-style prepared pizza crust (10 ounces)
1 can (12 ounces) tuna packed in water, drained
½ cup minced onion
⅓ cup reduced-fat mayonnaise
9 thin plum tomato slices
4 to 5 slices (¾ ounce each) process cheese
    food or American cheese

1. Preheat oven to 425°F. Place pizza crust on pizza pan or baking sheet.

2. Combine tuna, onion and mayonnaise in medium bowl; season to taste with salt and pepper. Stir until blended. Spread mixture over crust, leaving 1-inch border. Arrange tomato slices on tuna mixture in 3 rows, spacing at least ½ inch apart.

3. Bake 10 to 12 minutes or until heated through.

4. While pizza is baking, cut cheese slices into ½-inch-wide strips.

5. Remove pizza from oven. Arrange enough strips over tuna mixture to resemble tic-tac-toe game. Crisscross remaining strips over some tomato slices. Let stand 5 minutes before serving.

Makes 6 servings

Prep and Cook Time: 30 minutes

Tic-Tac-Toe Tuna Pizza

Campbell's® Chicken Quesadillas & Fiesta Rice

> 1 pound skinless, boneless chicken breasts, cubed
> 1 can (10¾ ounces) CAMPBELL'S® Condensed Cheddar Cheese Soup
> ½ cup PACE® Thick & Chunky Salsa *or* Picante Sauce (Medium)
> 10 flour tortillas (8-inch)
> Campbell's® Fiesta Rice (recipe follows)

1. Preheat oven to 425°F.

2. In medium nonstick skillet over medium-high heat, cook chicken 5 minutes or until no longer pink and juices evaporate, stirring often. Add soup and salsa. Heat to a boil, stirring occasionally.

3. Place tortillas on 2 baking sheets. Top **half** of each tortilla with **about ⅓ cup** soup mixture. Spread to within ½ inch of edge. Moisten edges of tortilla with water. Fold over and press edges together.

4. Bake 5 minutes or until hot.   *Makes 4 servings*

Campbell's® Fiesta Rice: In saucepan heat 1 can CAMPBELL'S® Condensed Chicken Broth, ½ cup water and ½ cup PACE® Thick & Chunky Salsa or Picante Sauce to a boil. Stir in 2 cups uncooked Minute® Original Rice. Cover and remove from heat. Let stand 5 minutes.

Prep/Cook Time: 20 minutes

Campbell's® Chicken Quesadillas
& Fiesta Rice

Sweet Treats

Sugar and spice and everything nice! That's what these yummy goodies are made of. Scrumptious cookies, cupcakes and desserts will tempt anyone who has eaten all their vegetables.

Dish of Dirt

14 OREO® Chocolate Sandwich Cookies, finely crushed (about 1 cup crumbs), divided
1 pint chocolate ice cream
¼ cup chocolate-flavored syrup
Gummy worms, for garnish
Prepared whipped topping, for garnish

In each of 4 dessert dishes, place 2 tablespoons cookie crumbs. Top each with ½ cup ice cream, remaining 2 tablespoons cookie crumbs and 1 tablespoon syrup. Garnish with gummy worms and whipped topping.

Makes 4 servings

Dish of Dirt

Peanut Butter and Jelly Sandwich Cookies

1 package (about 18 ounces) refrigerated sugar
    cookie dough
1 tablespoon unsweetened cocoa powder
    All-purpose flour (optional)
1¾ cups creamy peanut butter
½ cup grape jam or jelly

1. Remove dough from wrapper according to package directions. Reserve ¼ of dough; cover and refrigerate remaining ¾ of dough. Combine reserved dough and cocoa in small bowl; refrigerate.

2. Shape remaining ¾ dough into 5½-inch log. Sprinkle with flour to minimize sticking, if necessary. Remove chocolate dough from refrigerator; roll on sheet of waxed paper to 9½×6½-inch rectangle. Place dough log in center of rectangle.

3. Bring waxed paper edges and chocolate dough up and together over log. Press gently on top and sides of dough so entire log is wrapped in chocolate dough. Flatten log slightly to form square. Wrap in waxed paper. Freeze 10 minutes.

4. Preheat oven to 350°F. Remove waxed paper from dough. Cut dough into ¼-inch slices. Place slices 2 inches apart on ungreased cookie sheets. Reshape dough edges into square, if necessary. Press dough slightly to form indentation so dough resembles slice of bread.

5. Bake 8 to 11 minutes or until lightly browned. Remove from oven and straighten cookie edges with spatula. Cool 2 minutes on cookie sheets. Remove to wire racks; cool completely.

6. To make sandwich, spread about 1 tablespoon peanut butter on underside of 1 cookie. Spread about ½ tablespoon jam over peanut butter; top with second cookie, pressing gently. Repeat with remaining cookies. *Makes 11 sandwich cookies*

Peanut Butter and Jelly Sandwich Cookies

Baker's® One Bowl® G'me S'more Brownies!

9 whole graham crackers
4 squares BAKER'S® Unsweetened Baking
    Chocolate
¾ cup (1½ sticks) butter *or* margarine
2 cups sugar
3 eggs
1 teaspoon vanilla
1 cup flour
1 package (10½ ounces) miniature
    marshmallows
1 package (11 ounces) BAKER'S® Milk
    Chocolate Chips

HEAT oven to 350°F. Line bottom of greased 13×9-inch baking pan with graham crackers.

MICROWAVE chocolate and butter in large microwavable bowl on HIGH 2 minutes or until butter is melted. Stir until chocolate is completely melted.

STIR sugar into chocolate mixture until well blended. Mix in eggs and vanilla. Stir in flour until well blended. Spread over crackers in prepared pan.

BAKE 30 to 35 minutes or until toothpick inserted in center comes out with fudgy crumbs. *Do not overbake.* Sprinkle marshmallows and chocolate chips evenly over top of brownies. Return to oven 5 minutes or just until marshmallows begin to melt together. Cool completely. *Makes 24 brownies*

Tip: For ease in cutting, dip knife in warm water and wipe dry between cuts.

Prep Time: 10 minutes
Bake Time: 40 minutes

Hollywood Walk of Fame Stars

1 (12-ounce) package milk chocolate chips
1 (12-ounce) package butterscotch chips
½ cup PETER PAN® Crunchy Peanut Butter
1 bag popped ORVILLE REDENBACHER'S®
    REDENBUDDERS® MOVIE THEATER
    BUTTER POPPING CORN, unpopped
    kernels discarded
1 cup cornflakes cereal
1 cup honey graham cereal
    WESSON® No-Stick Cooking Spray
    Large star-shaped cookie cutter

1. Melt chocolate and butterscotch chips in large saucepan over low heat.

2. Stir in peanut butter until smooth. Remove from heat. Stir in popcorn, cornflakes and graham cereal. Coat evenly.

3. Line 15½×10-inch jelly roll pan with foil. Lightly spray with cooking spray.

4. Spread popcorn mixture evenly in pan. Refrigerate 15 minutes.

5. Spray cookie cutter with cooking spray.

6. Carefully press out stars. Store in refrigerator.

Makes 12 medium or 6 to 8 large stars

Total Preparation Time: 50 minutes

Ice Cream Cone Cakes

1 package (18¼ ounces) devil's food cake mix
   plus ingredients to prepare mix
⅓ cup sour cream
1 package flat-bottomed ice cream cones (about
   18 cones)
1¼ cups nonfat frozen yogurt (any flavor)
   Cake decorations or chocolate sprinkles

1. Preheat oven to 350°F. Grease and flour 8- or 9-inch round cake pan; set aside.

2. Prepare cake mix according to package directions, substituting sour cream for ⅓ cup of the water and decreasing oil to ¼ cup.

3. Spoon ½ of the batter (about 2⅓ cups) evenly into ice cream cones, using about 2 tablespoons batter for each. Pour remaining batter into prepared cake pan.

4. Stand cones on cookie sheet. Bake cones and cake layer until toothpick inserted into center of cake comes out clean, about 20 minutes for cones and about 35 minutes for cake layer. Cool on wire racks, removing cake from pan after 10 minutes. Reserve or freeze cake layer for another use.

5. Top each filled cone with ¼ cup scoop of frozen yogurt just before serving. Sprinkle with decorations as desired. Serve immediately. *Makes 18 servings*

Ice Cream Cone Cakes

Wild Side Sundaes

4 packages (4-serving size) JELL-O® Brand
　　Gelatin, 4 different flavors
4 cups boiling water
2 cups cold water
1 tub (8 ounces) COOL WHIP® Whipped
　　Topping, thawed
　Additional thawed COOL WHIP® Whipped
　　Topping

DISSOLVE each package of gelatin completely in 1 cup boiling water in separate bowls. Stir ½ cup cold water into each bowl of gelatin. Pour each mixture into separate 8-inch square pans. Refrigerate at least 3 hours or until firm. Cut gelatin in each pan into ½-inch cubes.

LAYER gelatin cubes alternately with whipped topping in sundae glasses. Garnish with dollop of additional whipped topping.

REFRIGERATE until ready to serve.　　　　　　*Makes 16 servings*

Wild Side Sundaes

Sweet Treats

Cookies & Cream Cupcakes

2¼ cups all-purpose flour
1 tablespoon baking powder
½ teaspoon salt
1⅔ cups sugar
½ cup butter, softened
1 cup milk
2 teaspoons vanilla
3 egg whites
1 cup crushed chocolate sandwich cookies
   (about 10 cookies) plus additional for
   garnish
1 (16 ounce) container prepared vanilla frosting

1. Preheat oven to 350°F. Line 24 regular-size (2½-inch) muffin pan cups with paper muffin cup liners.

2. Sift flour, baking powder and salt together in large bowl. Stir in sugar. Add butter, milk and vanilla; beat with electric mixer at low speed 30 seconds. Beat at medium speed 2 minutes. Add egg whites; beat 2 minutes. Stir in 1 cup crushed cookies.

3. Spoon batter into prepared muffin pans. Bake 20 to 25 minutes or until toothpick inserted into centers comes out clean. Cool in pans on wire racks 10 minutes. Remove to racks; cool completely.

4. Frost cupcakes; garnish with additional crushed cookies.

Makes 24 cupcakes

Cookies & Cream Cupcakes

Letters of the Alphabet

Gingerbread Cookie Dough (recipe follows)
Colored frostings and glazes, colored sugars,
sprinkles and assorted small candies

1. Prepare Gingerbread Cookie Dough. Cover; refrigerate about 8 hours or until firm.

2. Preheat oven to 350°F. Grease cookie sheets.

3. Divide dough into 4 equal sections. Reserve 1 section; refrigerate remaining 3 sections.

4. Roll reserved dough on well-floured surface to ⅛-inch thickness. Sprinkle with flour to minimize sticking, if necessary.

5. Cut out alphabet letter shapes using 2½-inch cookie cutters. Place cut out cookies on cookie sheet. Repeat steps with remaining dough.

6. Bake 6 to 8 minutes or until edges begin to brown. Remove cookies to wire racks; cool completely.

7. Decorate cookies with frostings, glazes, colored sugars, sprinkles and assorted small candies.   *Makes about 5 dozen cookies*

Gingerbread Cookie Dough

½ cup shortening
⅓ cup packed light brown sugar
¼ cup dark molasses
1 egg white
½ teaspoon vanilla
1½ cups all-purpose flour
1 teaspoon ground cinnamon
½ teaspoon baking soda
½ teaspoon salt
½ teaspoon ground ginger
¼ teaspoon baking powder

1. Beat shortening, brown sugar, molasses, egg white and vanilla in large bowl at high speed of electric mixer until smooth.

2. Combine flour, cinnamon, baking soda, salt, ginger and baking powder in small bowl. Add to shortening mixture; mix well. Cover; refrigerate about 8 hours or until firm.

Brownie Sandwich Cookies

BROWNIE COOKIES

1 package DUNCAN HINES® Chocolate Lovers
    Double Fudge Brownie Mix
1 egg
3 tablespoons water
Sugar

FILLING

1 container (16 ounces) DUNCAN HINES®
    Creamy Homestyle Cream Cheese Frosting
Red food coloring (optional)
½ cup semisweet mini chocolate chips

1. Preheat oven to 375°F. Grease cookie sheets.

2. For brownie cookies, combine brownie mix, fudge packet from mix, egg and water in large bowl. Stir until well blended, about 50 strokes. Shape dough into 50 (1-inch) balls. Place 2 inches apart on prepared cookie sheets. Grease bottom of drinking glass; dip in sugar. Press gently to flatten 1 cookie to ⅜-inch thickness. Repeat with remaining cookies. Bake at 375°F for 6 to 7 minutes or until set. Cool 1 minute on cookie sheets. Remove to cooling racks. Cool completely.

3. For filling, tint frosting with red food coloring, if desired. Stir in chocolate chips.

4. To assemble, spread 1 tablespoon frosting on bottom of one cookie; top with second cookie. Press together to make sandwich cookie. Repeat with remaining cookies.

Makes 25 sandwich cookies

Brownie Sandwich Cookies

Fruity Cookie Rings and Twists

1 package (20 ounces) refrigerated sugar cookie
    dough
3 cups fruit-flavored cereal, crushed and divided

1. Remove dough from wrapper according to package directions.

2. Combine dough and ½ cup cereal in large bowl. Divide dough into 32 balls. Refrigerate 1 hour.

3. Preheat oven to 375°F. Roll dough balls into 6- to 8-inch-long ropes. Roll ropes in remaining cereal to coat; shape into rings or fold in half and twist.

4. Place cookies 2 inches apart on ungreased cookie sheets.

5. Bake 10 to 11 minutes or until lightly browned. Remove to wire racks; cool completely.   *Makes 32 cookies*

Tip: These cookie rings can be transformed into Christmas tree ornaments by poking a hole in the unbaked ring using a drinking straw. Bake cookies and decorate with colored gels and small candies to resemble wreaths. Loop thin ribbon through holes and tie together.

Fruity Cookie Rings and Twists

Mud Slides

2 cups cold milk
1 package (4-serving size) JELL-O® Chocolate
    Flavor Instant Pudding & Pie Filling
14 chocolate sandwich cookies, finely crushed
    (about 1½ cups)
2 cups thawed COOL WHIP® Whipped Topping

LINE bottoms and sides of 2 loaf pans with wet paper towels. Tilt 2 (12-ounce) glasses in each pan.

POUR milk into 1-quart container with tight-fitting lid. Add pudding mix; cover tightly. Shake vigorously at least 45 seconds; pour evenly into glasses.

GENTLY stir 1¼ cups of the cookies into whipped topping with wire whisk in medium bowl until blended. Spoon evenly over pudding in glasses; sprinkle with remaining ¼ cup cookies.

REFRIGERATE until ready to serve. *Makes 4 servings*

Mud Slide

Perfect Parties

Looking for some new ideas for your child's next party? Choose from four fun menus with tasty recipes to make your tyke's next birthday or celebration easy for you and memorable for them.

- **Backyard Camp-out**
- **Slumber Party**
- **Fairy Princess Party**
- **Under the Sea Party**

Campfire Hot Dogs

½ pound ground beef
2 cups RAGÚ® Old World Style® Pasta Sauce
1 can (10¾ to 16 ounces) baked beans
8 frankfurters, cooked
8 frankfurter rolls

1. In 12-inch skillet, brown ground beef over medium-high heat; drain.

2. Stir in Ragú Pasta Sauce and beans. Bring to a boil over high heat. Reduce heat to low and simmer, stirring occasionally, 5 minutes.

3. To serve, arrange frankfurters in rolls and top with sauce mixture. Garnish, if desired, with Cheddar cheese.
Makes 8 servings

Tip: For Chili Campfire Hot Dogs, simply stir 2 to 3 teaspoon chili powder into sauce mixture.

Prep Time: 5 minutes
Cook Time: 10 minutes

BACKYARD CAMP-OUT

- Campfire Hot Dogs
- Campbell's Cheddary Pouch Potatoes
- S'mores

Campfire Hot Dogs

Campbell's® Cheddary Pouch Potatoes

1 can (10¾ ounces) CAMPBELL'S® Condensed
   Cheddar Cheese Soup
¼ cup milk
½ teaspoon garlic powder
¼ teaspoon onion powder
4 cups frozen steak fries
   Paprika

1. In large bowl mix soup, milk, garlic powder and onion powder. Stir in potatoes.

2. Cut four 14-inch squares of heavy-duty aluminum foil. Spoon *1 cup* soup mixture onto each square, arranging potatoes to make a single layer. Sprinkle with paprika. Bring up sides of foil and double fold. Double fold ends to make packet.

3. Place potato packets on grill rack over medium-hot coals. Grill 25 minutes or until potatoes are tender. *Makes 4 servings*

Campbell's® Cheddary Oven Pouch Potatoes: In Step 3, on baking sheet bake packets at 350°F. for 25 minutes.

Prep Time: 5 minutes
Cook Time: 25 minutes

S'Mores

16 graham cracker squares
4 milk chocolate bars (1.55 ounces each),
    halved
1 cup miniature marshmallows

1. Preheat broiler.

2. Arrange half of graham crackers on baking sheet. Top each cracker with 1 piece of the chocolate bars. Broil until chocolate is softened but not melted.

3. Arrange 2 tablespoons marshmallows on each cracker. Broil until lightly toasted.

4. Top with remaining crackers and serve.   *Makes 8 s'mores*

Campbell's® Cheddary Pouch Potatoes

Smushy Cookies

1 package (20 ounces) refrigerated cookie
     dough, any flavor
All-purpose flour (optional)
Peanut butter, multi-colored miniature
     marshmallows, assorted colored sprinkles,
     chocolate-covered raisins and caramel candy
     squares

1. Preheat oven to 350°F. Grease cookie sheets.

2. Remove dough from wrapper according to package directions.
Cut into 4 equal sections. Reserve 1 section; refrigerate remaining 3
sections.

3. Roll reserved dough to ¼-inch thickness. Sprinkle with flour to
minimize sticking, if necessary. Cut out cookies using 2½-inch round
cookie cutter. Transfer to prepared cookie sheets. Repeat with
remaining dough, working with 1 section at a time.

4. Bake 8 to 11 minutes or until edges are light golden brown.
Remove to wire racks; cool completely.

5. To make sandwich, spread about 1½ tablespoons peanut butter
on underside of 1 cookie to within ¼ inch of edge. Sprinkle with
miniature marshmallows and candy pieces. Top with second cookie,
pressing gently. Repeat with remaining cookies and fillings.

6. Just before serving, place sandwiches on paper towels. Microwave
at HIGH 15 to 25 seconds or until fillings become soft.

Makes about 8 to 10 sandwich cookies

SLUMBER PARTY

- Chili Chip Party Platter
- Cinnamon RedHot® Popcorn
- Smushy Cookies

Smushy Cookies

Chili Chip Party Platter

1 pound ground beef
1 medium onion, chopped
1 package (1.48 ounces) LAWRY'S® Spices
    & Seasonings for Chili
1 can (6 ounces) tomato paste
1 cup water
1 bag (8 to 9 ounces) tortilla chips or corn chips
1½ cups (6 ounces) shredded cheddar cheese
1 can (2¼ ounces) sliced pitted black olives,
    drained
½ cup sliced green onions

In medium skillet, cook ground beef until browned and crumbly; drain fat. Add onion, Spices & Seasonings for Chili, tomato paste and water; mix well. Bring to a boil over medium-high heat. Reduce heat to low; simmer, uncovered, 15 minutes, stirring occasionally. Serve over tortilla chips. Top with cheddar cheese, olives and green onion.

Serving Suggestion: Serve with a cool beverage and sliced melon.

Chili Chip Party Platter

Cinnamon RedHot® Popcorn

10 cups air-popped popcorn (½ cup unpopped)
1½ cups (7 ounces) coarsely chopped pecans
¾ cup granulated sugar
¾ cup packed light brown sugar
½ cup light corn syrup
3 tablespoons *Frank's® RedHot®* Sauce
2 tablespoons honey
6 tablespoons (¾ stick) unsalted butter, at room
   temperature, cut into thin pats
1 tablespoon ground cinnamon

1. Preheat oven to 250°F. Place popcorn and pecans in 5-quart ovenproof bowl or Dutch oven. Bake 15 minutes.

2. Combine sugars, corn syrup, **RedHot** Sauce and honey in 2-quart saucepan. Bring to a full boil over medium-high heat, stirring just until sugars dissolve. Boil about 6 to 8 minutes or until soft crack stage (290°F on candy thermometer). *Do not stir.* Remove from heat.

3. Gradually add butter and cinnamon to sugar mixture, stirring gently until well blended. Pour over popcorn, tossing to coat evenly.* Spread popcorn mixture on greased baking sheets, using two forks. Cool completely. Break into bite-size pieces. Store in airtight container up to 2 weeks. *Makes 18 cups*

*If popcorn mixture sets too quickly, return to oven to rewarm. Popcorn mixture may be shaped into 3-inch balls while warm, if desired.

Prep Time: 15 minutes
Cook Time: 8 to 10 minutes

Cinnamon RedHot® Popcorn

Dream Castle

5¼ cups Buttercream Frosting (page 86)
   Blue and yellow food color
3 (8-inch) square cakes, tops and edges trimmed
2 cups Base Frosting (page 86), if desired
   Assorted colored sugar
4 sugar ice cream cones
   Small purple and white gumdrops
   Pastel candy-coated chocolate pieces
2 pink sugar wafer cookies
1 (19×13-inch) cake board, cut in half crosswise
   and covered

1. Color ½ cup Buttercream Frosting blue and ½ cup yellow; reserve 4¼ cups white frosting. Place one square cake on prepared cake board. Frost top with some of the white frosting.

2. Cut remaining cakes as shown in diagrams 1 and 2 (see page 86).

3. Place piece A over bottom layer. Frost top of piece A with some of the white frosting. Position remaining pieces as shown in diagram 3 (see page 86), connecting with some of the white frosting.

4. Frost entire cake with Base Frosting to seal in crumbs. Frost again with white frosting. Cover piece D (bridge) with colored sugar.

5. Frost cones with blue and yellow frostings. Place as shown.

6. Decorate as shown, using frosting to attach candies, if needed. Arrange wafer cookies on front of castle for gate.

Makes 24 to 28 servings

Continued on page 86

Dream Castle

Dream Castle, *continued*

Buttercream Frosting

6 cups powdered sugar, sifted and divided
¾ cup butter or margarine, softened
¼ cup shortening
6 to 8 tablespoons milk, divided
1 teaspoon vanilla extract

Place 3 cups sugar, butter, shortening, 4 tablespoons milk and vanilla in large bowl. Beat with electric mixer until smooth. Add remaining 3 cups powdered sugar; beat at medium speed until light and fluffy, adding more milk, 1 tablespoon at a time, as needed for good spreading consistency. *Makes about 3½ cups frosting*

Base Frosting

3 cups powdered sugar, sifted
½ cup shortening
¼ cup milk, plus additional, if necessary
½ teaspoon vanilla

Combine sugar, shortening, ¼ cup milk and vanilla in large bowl. Beat with electric mixer on medium speed until smooth. Add more milk, 1 teaspoon at a time, until frosting is a thin consistency. Use frosting immediately. *Makes about 2 cups*

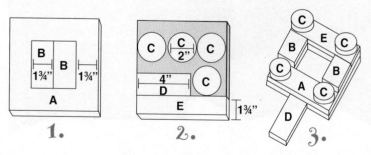

Magic Wands

1 cup semisweet chocolate chips
12 pretzel rods
3 ounces white chocolate baking bars or almond
**   bark**
Red and yellow food color
Assorted sprinkles

1. Line baking sheet with waxed paper.

2. Melt semisweet chocolate in top of double boiler over hot, not boiling, water. Remove from heat. Dip pretzel rods into chocolate, spooning chocolate to coat about ¾ of each pretzel. Place on prepared baking sheet. Refrigerate until chocolate is firm.

3. Melt white chocolate in top of clean double boiler over hot, not boiling, water. Stir in food colors to make orange. Remove from heat. Dip coated pretzels quickly into colored chocolate to coat about ¼ of each pretzel.

4. Place on baking sheet. Immediately top with sprinkles. Refrigerate until chocolate is firm.

5. Tie ends with ribbons. *Makes 12 wands*

Octo-Dogs and Shells

4 hot dogs
1½ cups uncooked small shell pasta
1½ cups frozen mixed vegetables
1 cup prepared Alfredo sauce
Prepared yellow mustard in squeeze bottle
Cheese-flavored fish-shaped crackers

Lay 1 hot dog on side with end facing you. Starting 1 inch from one end of hot dog, slice hot dog vertically in half. Roll hot dog ¼ turn and slice in half vertically again, making 4 segments connected at the top. Slice each segment in half vertically, creating a total of 8 "legs." Repeat with remaining hot dogs.

Place hot dogs in medium saucepan; cover with water. Bring to a boil over medium-high heat. Remove from heat; set aside.

Prepare pasta according to package directions, stirring in vegetables during last 3 minutes of cooking time. Drain; return to pan. Stir in Alfredo sauce. Heat over low heat until heated through. Divide pasta mixture between four plates.

Drain "octo-dogs." Arrange one octo-dog on top of pasta mixture on each plate. Draw faces on "heads" of octo-dogs with mustard. Sprinkle crackers over pasta mixture.   *Makes 4 servings*

UNDER THE SEA

- Octo-Dogs and Shells
- blue gelatin blocks with gummy fish
- School-of-Fish Cake

Octo-Dog and Shells

School-of-Fish Cake

1 (13×9-inch) cake
1 recipe Creamy White Frosting (page 92)
  Blue paste food coloring
1 recipe Base Frosting (page 86)
  Large and small gumdrops
1 (19×13-inch) cake board, cut to fit cake if
    desired, covered

1. If cake top is rounded, trim horizontally with long serrated knife. Trim sides of cake. Place cake on prepared cake board.

2. Tint Creamy White Frosting blue by adding small amount of desired paste color with toothpick; stir well. Slowly add more color until frosting is desired shade.

3. Frost top and sides of cake with Base Frosting to seal in crumbs. Frost again with blue frosting. Swirl frosting to resemble waves.

4. To make large fish, position 1 large gumdrop on cutting board and cut lengthwise in half. Set aside 1 gumdrop half for fish body. For tail, place remaining gumdrop half, cut side down, on cutting board. Cut wedge piece from center of wide end (see photo 1, page 92). Place fish body in desired position on cake top. Place narrow end of tail piece next to wide end of fish body (see photo 2, page 92). Trim reserved wedge piece into fin shape and place above body of fish.

5. For eyes and bubbles, cut off small pieces of gumdrop and press onto fish and cake. Decorate fish by cutting additional small pieces of gumdrop and pressing pieces onto fish, if desired. Repeat with additional large gumdrops to make more large fish. Repeat with small gumdrops to make small fish.   *Makes 16 to 20 servings*

Continued on page 92

School-of-Fish Cake

School-of-Fish Cake, continued

1. Trim piece into
   fin shape.

2. Place tail next to
   fish body.

Creamy White Frosting

½ cup shortening
6 cups sifted powdered sugar, divided
3 tablespoons milk
2 teaspoons clear vanilla extract
Additional milk*

For thinner frosting, use more milk and for thicker frosting use less milk.

Beat shortening in large bowl with electric mixer at medium speed until fluffy. Gradually beat in 3 cups sugar until well blended and smooth. Carefully beat in 3 tablespoons milk and vanilla. Gradually beat in remaining 3 cups sugar, adding more milk, 1 teaspoon at a time, as needed for good spreading consistency. Store in refrigerator.

Makes enough to fill and frost 2 (8-inch) round or square cake layers or frost 1 (13×9-inch) cake

Acknowledgments

The publisher would like to thank the companies and organizations listed below for the use of their recipes and photographs in this publication.

Bestfoods
Bob Evans®
Campbell Soup Company
ConAgra Grocery Products Company
Dole Food Company, Inc.
Duncan Hines® and Moist Deluxe® are registered trademarks of Aurora Foods Inc.
Egg Beaters®
The Golden Grain Company®
Hershey Foods Corporation
Hormel Foods Corporation
The HV Company
Kraft Foods, Inc.
Lawry's® Foods, Inc.
Lipton®
National Honey Board
North Dakota Beef Commission
OREO® Cookies
Reckitt Benckiser
The J.M. Smucker Company
StarKist® Seafood Company
Texas Peanut Producers Board
Uncle Ben's Inc.

Index

Index

Index